Shakespeare for Students, Second Edition, Volume 1

Project Editor
Anne Marie Hacht

Rights Acquisition and Management
Lisa Kincade, Robbie McCord, Lista Person, Kelly Quin, and Andrew Specht

Manufacturing
Rita Wimberley

Imaging
Lezlie Light

Product Design
Pamela A. E. Galbreath and Jennifer Wahi

Vendor Administration
Civie Green

Product Manager
Meggin Condino

LIBRARY OF CONGRESS CATALOGING-IN-PUBLICATION DATA

Shakespeare for students: critical interpretations of Shakespeare's plays and poetry.-2nd ed. / Anne Marie Hacht, editor; foreword by Cynthia Burnstein.

p. cm.

Includes bibliographical references and index.

ISBN-13: 978-1-4144-1255-9 (set)
ISBN-10: 1-4144-1255-X (set)
ISBN-13: 978-1-4144-1256-6 (v. 1)
ISBN-10: 1-4144-1256-8 (v. 1)
[etc.]

1. Shakespeare, William, 1564–1616—Outlines, syllabi, *etc.* 2. Shakespeare, William, 1564–1616—Criticism and interpretation. 3. Shakespeare, William, 1564–1616—Examinations-Study guides. I. Hacht, Anne Marie.

PR2987.S47 2007

822.3'3—dc22 2007008901

ISBN-13
978-1-4144-1255-9 (set)
978-1-4144-1256-6 (vol. 1)
978-1-4144-1258-0 (vol. 2)
978-1-4144-1259-7 (vol. 3)

ISBN-10
1-1444-1255-X (set)
1-4144-1256-8 (vol. 1)
1-4144-1258-4 (vol. 2)
1-4144-1259-2 (vol. 3)

This title is also available as an e-book.
ISBN-13 978-1-4144-2937-3 (set) ISBN-10 1-4144-2937-1 (set)
Contact your Gale, an imprint of Cengage Learning sales representative for ordering information.

Printed in the United States of America

10 9 8 7 6 5 4 3 2 1

All's Well That Ends Well

William Shakespeare

1603

All's Well That Ends Well was probably written sometime between 1600 and 1605, and many experts date the work to 1603. Others believe that the play is the lost Shakespearean drama titled *Love's Labour Won*, which was written before 1598. The first written mention of the play under its current title appeared in 1623, when it was licensed to be printed in Shakespeare's Folio. Attempts to date the play have involved a bit of detective work regarding some of its language, particularly Helen's letter to the countess in act 3, which exemplifies Shakespeare's less-sophisticated early style. Conversely, some critics note similarities between the tone and style of the play with that of *Measure for Measure*, which was written in 1604. Some commentators have theorized that the uneven nature of the play suggests that it was written at two different times in Shakespeare's life. This sketchy history indicates that the play did not attract much attention when it was first written and performed, a testament to its status as a lesser work in Shakespeare's canon.

All's Well That Ends Well has often been called one of Shakespeare's problem plays or dark comedies, a category that usually includes *Measure for Measure* and *Troilus and Cressida*. The problem refers to the cynical nature of the plot's resolution, in which Bertram, a rather unbecoming hero who is sought after by a woman who is too good for him, has a last-minute change of heart and vows to love Helena, his wife, forever. This declaration comes on the heels of a rather devious scheme and is not prompted by a personal revelation deep enough to be convincing to the audience. The problem plays are more similar in tone and theme to Shakespeare's tragedies than they are to his romantic comedies.

Shakespeare's primary inspiration for the plot of *All's Well That Ends Well* was William Painter's collection of stories *The Palace of Pleasures* (1575), which itself was an English translation of "Giletta of Narbonne," a story in Giovanni Boccaccio's collection of folk tales called the

Decameron (1353). Shakespeare fleshed out the story by adding the characters of Parolles, the Countess of Rossillion, Lavache, and Lafew. The events of the play, in which a low-born woman schemes to marry a count and wins both his ring and his child by switching places with another woman during an illicit rendezvous (a tactic known as the bed-trick), has its roots in folk tales. This may account, some believe, for the play's unbelievable nature and thus its failure as a comedy. Others believe that audiences of the day would have been familiar with such folk tales, as well as with Painter's *The Palace of Pleasures* and Boccaccio's *Decameron*, and thus would have received the play more warmly. That said, nearly all critics have at least some reservations about it.

Early critics of the play focused their attention on the incongruous plot elements and the themes of merit and rank, virtue and honor, and male versus female. More recent critics also address these issues, but they focus more attention on topics such as gender and desire. Helena's bold sexuality and her reversal of gender roles, in which she is the pursuer rather than the pursued, has generated much discussion, especially for how they intertwine with other main conflicts in the play, such as social class, the bed-trick, and marriage. Whether the play does end well, as the title suggests, has also historically been much debated.

The three main characters—Helena, Bertram, and Parolles—have generated a great deal of literary criticism over the years. Some critics brand Helena as conniving and obsessive in her love for Bertram, while others find her virtuous and noble. In general, critics are not fond of the character of Bertram, though some judge him more harshly than others. Some critics find him thoroughly unrepentant and unredeemable at the end of the play, making the ending implausible. Others are more sympathetic toward him, finding him merely immature at the beginning of the play and in need of life experience, which he obtains while fighting in Florence. Parolles has generated less controversy in terms of the nature of his character (even Parolles himself recognizes his deficiencies and is not ashamed of them), and some critics find the subplot involving Parolles the only thing that saves the play from failure.

There is no record of *All's Well That Ends Well* having been performed in Shakespeare's time (although it probably was), and it remained unpopular for several hundred years. In England, it was performed only a few dozen times in the eighteenth century and only seventeen times in the nineteenth century. The Victorians abhorred the sexual nature of the play. Writing in 1852, critic John Bull (quoted in the New Cambridge edition of the play edited by Russell Fraser) found that such wantonness cannot "be made presentable to an audience of which decent females form a portion." In the United States, the play was not staged until well into the twentieth century. In most cases, when it was performed, many changes were made to the text to make it more contemporary, often highlighting Parolles's part and turning the play into a farce.

Act 1, Scene 1

All's Well That Ends Well opens at the palace in Rossillion, a region in France that borders Spain and the Mediterranean Sea. Here, the Countess of Rossillion mourns her recently deceased husband and the imminent departure of her son, Bertram, the Count of Rossillion, who has been summoned to Paris by the king. The countess and her friend, the elderly Lord Lafew, discuss the king's poor health and lament that Gerard de Narbon, a famous court doctor who has just died, is not around to heal him. The doctor's daughter, the beautiful and vivacious Helena, has become the countess's ward.

In a soliloquy, Helena reveals her love for Bertram. Because she is a commoner, there is no hope of them being together, and yet she cannot bear the thought of his departure. Parolles, Bertram's best friend, whom Helena acknowledges is a liar and a coward, enters and engages Helena in a coarse conversation about the pros and cons of her virginity. Helena intends to protect her virginity, but Parolles urges her to give it up. To him it is a wasted virtue, particularly once a woman becomes a certain age. The conversation prompts Helena to take matters into her own hands. Her love for Bertram can be realized only through her own actions, and not by waiting for something to happen: "Our remedies oft in ourselves do lie, / Which we ascribe to heaven," she says.

Act 1, Scene 2

In Paris, the King of France confers with two lords, the Brothers Dumaine, about the dispute between Sienna and Florence; he states that he will allow his soldiers to fight on either side. Bertram, Parolles, and Lafew enter, and the king welcomes them, reminiscing fondly about Bertram's father, and wishing that Gerard de Narbon were still alive to cure his fistula.

Act 1, Scene 3

Back in Rossillion, the countess confers with Lavatch, a morose and ribald clown. The countess calls him a knave (stupid) and urges him to marry the servant woman he has gotten pregnant. She then asks her steward to fetch Helena. The steward tells the countess that he has overhead Helena talking to herself about her love for Bertram. When the lovesick Helena appears, the countess comments sympathetically on the girl's emotional state, for she was once young and in love.

The countess tells Helena that she loves her like a daughter, but Helena objects. If the countess were her mother, then Bertram would be her brother. Initially, Helena states that she cannot be the countess's daughter because she is a servant, and Bertram is a lord; they cannot be equals. The countess urges Helena to admit her real objection—that having feelings for her own brother would be improper—and she does. Helena also admits that she has plans to follow Bertram to Paris in order to try her father's cures on the king. The countess is doubtful; she says that the king's doctors have told him nothing can be done. Helena objects; she bets her life that she can cure the king. The countess relents and sends her off to Paris.

Act 2, Scene 1

In Paris, the king bids farewell to the Brothers Dumaine, who are off to fight for Florence in the war with Sienna. Lafew announces the arrival of Gerard de Narbon's daughter, Helena, who has come to cure the ailing king. Helena explains that upon his deathbed, her father passed on his knowledge to her. The king doubts her ability to make him better, but she swears upon her life that he will be healed within a day or two. She offers a wager: If she fails, she will be put to death; if she succeeds, she will be able to choose her own husband from among "the royal blood of France." With little conviction, the king accepts her offer.

Act 2, Scene 2

The countess entrusts Lavatch with the task of traveling to Paris to give Helena a note and check up on Bertram. In a series of bawdy comments that frustrate the countess, Lavatch agrees.

Act 2, Scene 3

Bertram, Parolles, and Lafew are stunned to see the king miraculously cured. The king urges Helena to have a seat and take her pick of husbands from the assembled gathering of lords. Lafew wishes he were younger so Helena might pick him. Helena addresses the lords, claiming to be a simple maid, and all refuse her. Then she decides on Bertram. "This is the man," she says. Bertram argues with the king on account of the fact that she is "a poor physician's daughter." The king responds that "From lowest place, whence virtuous things proceed, / The place is dignified by th'doer's deed." Furthermore, she is pretty and smart, and Bertram should be happy to have her. As for her lack of wealth and the social status, the king states that he is capable of granting them.

Bertram reiterates that he will never love her. Helena briefly recants her decision, but the king will not hear of it. His reputation is at stake, so he forces Bertram to marry her that night.

When the others have departed, Lafew and Parolles talk about what Lafew perceives as Parolles's lack of loyalty to Bertram. Lafew also derides Parolles's pompous personality and gaudy clothes. Parolles dismisses Lafew as an old man with no wisdom to impart. Lafew warns that such foolishness will lead Parolles to ruin. Offstage, Helena and Bertram are married. When Lafew tells Parolles that he has a new mistress (Helena), Parolles responds that he has no mistress and no lord other than God. Lafew responds that the devil is his master and that he should be beaten.

After Lafew leaves, Bertram enters. Bertram says that he will never consummate his marriage to Helena. Instead, he will go off to fight in the Tuscan wars and send Helena back to Rossillion. Parolles agrees to join him.

Act 2, Scene 4

Lavatch arrives in Paris and greets Helena and Parolles, whom he insults by calling him a knave. Parolles does not realize Lavatch has insulted him. Parolles tells Helena to prepare for her wedding night, and she leaves to await Bertram.

Act 2, Scene 5

Lafew tries to convince Bertram that Parolles will not be a trustworthy ally in battle, to no avail. Helena reappears, and Bertram tells her that he will not sleep with her that night because of his prior obligations. He gives her a letter to give to his mother and tells her to return to Rossillion. Helena vows that as his obedient servant she will do what he asks. After she leaves, Bertram confesses to Parolles that he will never return to her, and they go off to battle.

Act 3, Scene 1

In Florence, the duke addresses his troops,

which include the Brothers Dumaine, who are both serving as captains. The duke is perturbed that the king of France has not sided exclusively with him in the war, but the two lords proclaim their allegiance to the duke nonetheless.

Act 3, Scene 2

Lavatch returns to Rossillion and delivers Bertram's letter to the countess. The letter states that Bertram has been forced to marry Helena against his will. He has run away and plans never to return to the palace. The countess is angry that he is dishonoring both the king and Helena, whom she calls "a maid too virtuous / For the contempt of empire."

Helena arrives in Rossillion with the Brothers Dumaine. She realizes that Bertram is gone for good when the two lords tell the countess that Bertram has gone to battle for the Duke of Florence. Helena reads a passage from Bertram's letter, which states that she can only be his wife if she wears his ring (which he has refused to give her) and bears him a child. Furthermore, he says that as long as Helena is alive in France, he shall not return. The countess renounces him as her son.

In a soliloquy, Helena laments her position. She is sad for herself, but also worried that Bertram will be hurt or killed in battle. She decides to leave France so Bertram can return home safely.

Act 3, Scene 3

In a brief scene, the Duke of Florence leads Bertram and others into battle. Bertram bravely heads up the troops, and Parolles, coward that he is, follows in the rear.

Act 3, Scene 4

In Rossillion, the countess receives a letter from Helena stating that she has gone on a pilgrimage to the burial site of Saint Jacques le Grand (St. James the Greater) in hopes that her departure will prompt Bertram to return home. The countess urges her steward to write to Bertram in an effort to extol Helena's virtues and point out how childish he is being in refusing her as his wife. The countess thinks that if Bertram returns home and Helena hears about it, then she will return as well due to her immense desire to be near him.

Act 3, Scene 5

In the city of Florence, the Widow Capilet and her daughter, Diana, discuss the war. News of the young Count Bertram's heroism on the battlefield has spread fast, and they are aware of his brave deeds. However, Parolles has been seeking a female companion for the count and has spied Diana. Both the Widow and her friend Mariana warn Diana vehemently against becoming involved in an affair. If Diana loses her virginity to the Count of Rossillion, she will be ruined.

Helena arrives at the Widow's house in search of a place to stay on her pilgrimage to Saint Jacques le Grand. The Widow welcomes her and says that the Count of Rossillion, a war hero, is in town. Helena says she does not know him, but finds him handsome. Diana says that the count should not be so mean to his wife, but that Parolles should be poisoned.

Act 3, Scene 6

At the camp, the Brothers Dumaine try to convince Bertram that Parolles is a scoundrel, liar, and coward. Bertram doubts that they can prove such accusations. The lords offer to pose as the enemy, capture and blindfold Parolles, bring him back to the tents, and interrogate him, knowing full well that he will incriminate Bertram to save his own skin. Bertram agrees to the plan. Parolles enters the tent, stating his intent to find a prized regimental drum that was lost in battle. The others tell him to forget about it, but he is adamant, believing he will be deemed a hero for retrieving it. They relent, deciding that it will be the perfect time to capture him. Parolles proclaims he will attempt the dangerous maneuver that night.

Act 3, Scene 7

Helena convinces the Widow that she is the count's wife. She proposes a plan in which Diana's virtue will be spared by switching places with Diana during her scheduled rendezvous with Bertram.

Thus, Bertram will be sleeping unknowingly with his wife, not Diana. Ahead of time, Diana will ask that Bertram give her his ring and that neither of them speak for the hour they are together. The Widow agrees to the plan, because it will allow her daughter to retain her chastity. To seal the deal, Helena offers a great deal of money to Diana so that she will have a significant dowry and will be able to find herself a worthy husband afterward.

Act 4, Scene 1

Parolles arrives in a field, ostensibly on his quest to find the drum, but he has no intentions of doing so. Instead, he plans to take a nap, feign some injuries, and return to camp with a story about his brave but unsuccessful exploit. The two lords are hiding in the bushes, and they jump out, throwing a sack over his head. They have an interpreter utter some mumbo jumbo—"Boskos thromuldo boskos"—to make Parolles believe he has been captured by the foreign enemy. Parolles immediately offers to spill the beans about his army's secrets in an effort to spare his life. His "captors" agree to take him to their general, so Parolles can tell him everything.

Act 4, Scene 2

In his effort to plan his conquest, Bertram tries to seduce Diana by comparing her to the Greek goddess Diana and saying that remaining chaste would be a waste of her beauty. Diana reminds him that he is married, but Bertram brushes it off. He says he loves only Diana. Diana is not convinced; she knows that he just wants to sleep with her. She declares that she will believe his declaration of love only if he backs it up with the promise to marry her after his wife dies and if he gives her the family ring he wears on his finger. He protests, but gives in fairly quickly. Diana says she will meet him at midnight in her room. He will stay for only one hour, and neither of them will speak. In return for his ring, she will give him one of her own in return. After Bertram leaves, Diana gives a short soliloquy stating that her mother was right about him. All men are the same; they will promise anything to get a woman into bed.

Act 4, Scene 3

The Brothers Dumaine discuss Bertram. The first lord tells the second lord that Helena is dead, having succumbed to grief on her pilgrimage to Saint Jacques le Grand. Her death was confirmed by the priest of the shrine. Furthermore, Bertram knew this when he made his deal with Diana. The lords are saddened by Helena's death, and they are dismayed (but not surprised) that Bertram is cheered by it and happily announces that he will return to Rossillion shortly.

The two lords tell Bertram that Parolles has been held in the stocks, offering his "captors" a litany of confessions. Bertram still does not believe Parolles would say anything bad about him. To prove him wrong, Parolles is sent in, still blindfolded. Parolles says that the duke's horses are weak, his troops scattered, and his commanders are poor rogues. He further indicts Captain Dumaine as a low-level apprentice who once impregnated a mentally retarded girl. One of the captors retrieves a letter from Parolles's pocket, in which he wrote that Bertram is a fool. He claims to have been warning Diana that the count was "a dangerous and lascivious boy, who is a whale to virginity, and devours up all the fry it finds." He begs for his life and continues to say terrible things about Captain Dumaine, including that "drunkenness is his best virtue." He also condemns the other Captain Dumaine and readily agrees to betray all of them if only he is allowed to live. Bertram is livid at Parolles's betrayal. When Parolles is unmasked, he balks at being fooled but readily apologizes.

Act 4, Scene 4

Following the bed-trick (which takes place offstage), Helena tells the Widow and Diana that they will all return to France in order to make good on her promise. When they get there, Diana will need to do one more thing before their scheme is complete. Diana vows to do whatever Helena desires, such is her gratitude for having her virtue saved by the bed-trick. Helena assures her that "all's well that ends well."

Act 4, Scene 5

In Rossillion, Lafew criticizes Parolles, and the countess wishes she had never known him. She laments Helena's death, stating that she loved her as if she were her own child. Lafew proposes that Bertram marry his daughter, and the countess agrees. Lavatch engages in some off-color banter with Lafew and the countess; they both state that he is morose but harmless. Lavatch announces that Bertram has returned.

Act 5, Scene 1

While traveling to Rossillion as fast as they can, Helena, Diana, and the Widow encounter a gentleman. Helena asks him to take a message to the King of France. The gentleman states that the king is not in Paris but in fact heading for Rossillion. "All's well that ends well yet," Helena reminds the Widow. Helena promises a reward to the gentleman if he can deliver her letter to the king promptly, and he obliges.

Act 5, Scene 2

Parolles returns to Rossillion and urges Lavatch, who roundly criticizes Parolles's withered clothes and body odor, to give Lafew a letter. But Lafew enters, and Lavatch introduces Parolles as a "poor, decayed … foolish, rascally knave." Parolles begs forgiveness from Lafew, who grants it.

Act 5, Scene 3

The king mourns Helena's death, and with Lafew and the countess present, he summons Bertram. The king asks Bertram if he knows Lafew's daughter. The count says he was in love with her, and the king announces their betrothal. Lafew asks Bertram for a ring to give his daughter. He presents the ring he believes Diana gave him during their rendezvous. Lafew instantly recognizes it as Helena's ring, but Bertram objects. He claims it was thrown from a window by a woman who wanted to sleep with him. The king sides with Lafew, saying that Helena promised only to take it off her finger if she consummated her marriage with Bertram. Bertram remains adamant—he did not receive the ring from Helena. The king orders Bertram to be taken away. As Bertram is being led away, he says that if the ring belonged to Helena, then she, in fact, became his wife in Florence, and yet, she was not there, so the ring was not hers and she is not his wife.

Bertram is led away, and the king is perplexed. Meanwhile, the gentleman arrives with a letter to the king from Diana. The letter claims that Bertram promised to marry her upon the death of his wife, but that he fled Florence without making good on that promise. She is on her way to Rossillion to seek justice.

At this turn of events, Lafew recants his daughter's hand in marriage, believing Bertram not worthy of being her husband. The king agrees and starts to believe that Helena met with foul play, possibly at Bertram's hands. Bertram and Diana, along with her mother, are brought to court. The king asks Bertram if he knows either Diana or her mother, and Bertram refuses to answer, but states that Diana is not his wife. Diana insists that Bertram believes he took her virginity. Bertram says she was a whore. Diana presents his ring as proof that she is telling the truth. The countess and the king instantly believe her. Diana says that Parolles can vouch for her story, and he is ordered to appear. Bertram backtracks, saying he slept with Diana and she stole the ring. Diana says that she gave Bertram the ring the king is now wearing.

Bertram finally confesses; Parolles appears and confesses that he was the go-between for Bertram and Diana. The king questions Diana about the ring some more, and she cryptically says she never gave it to Bertram. The king knows full well the ring was Helena's and orders Diana to be sent to jail for refusing to cooperate. She sends her mother to fetch her bail.

Diana enjoys the riddle she has presented, and knowing of Helena's ensuing pregnancy, she tells the king: "Dead though she be, she feels her young one kick. So there's my riddle: one that's dead is quick."

The Widow presents Helena, who quotes Bertram's original letter: "When from my finger you can get this ring, / And are by me with child," proving that she has achieved Bertram's seemingly unattainable criteria. Presented with this evidence, Bertram professes his undying love for Helena and promises to be a faithful husband. The king, delighted at this turnabout, applauds Diana for retaining her chastity while allowing Helena to fulfill her role as Bertram's wife. He offers Diana a dowry and her choice for a husband.

Bertram, Count of Rossillion

Bertram is the Count of Rossillion. His father has recently died, and his mother, the Countess of Rossillion, is still in mourning. Bertram is quite young, perhaps no more than twenty, and he is eager to join the king's ranks in Paris and then go off to battle in Florence. Bertram's best friend is Parolles, but he is oblivious to the fact that Parolles is an opportunist and a scoundrel. Bertram balks at marrying Helena because she is a commoner with no wealth or status. He agrees reluctantly only after the king promises to endow Helena with wealth and a title in order to sweeten the deal. This is evidence of Bertram's snobbishness, as Helena's social standing outranks all her other positive qualities in Bertram's eyes. Finding himself trapped in a marriage to Helena, whom he does not love, he flees to Florence to join the wars. While there, he proves himself valiant on the battlefield, and his reputation as a hero spreads quickly throughout the city. He spies Diana in town and sends Parolles to set up a rendezvous. Before their scheduled tryst, he promises the young virgin that he truly loves her and will marry her as soon as his wife dies. That night, he believes he sleeps with her, but he beds his wife, Helena, instead. Thinking he is with Diana, he gives her his family ring as a token of his affection.

Media Adaptations

- *All's Well That Ends Well*, directed by John Barton and Claude Whatham and produced by the Royal Shakespeare Company, was filmed in 1968 by the BBC and released on video. The production stars Lynn Farleigh, Ian Richardson, and Catherine Lacey.

- *All's Well That Ends Well*, a 1981 production directed by Elijah Moshinsky and starring Ian Charleson, Angela Down, and Celia Johnson, was released by BBC Time/Life Series and distributed by Ambrose Video.

- An audiobook of *All's Well That Ends Well*, read by William Hutt and published as part of the CBC Stratford Festival Reading Series, is available on compact disc.

- A two-cassette full-cast recording of *All's Well That Ends Well*, starring Claire Bloom and Lynn Redgrave, was released by Caedmon Audio.

Bertram's first change of heart takes place when he witnesses the blindfolded Parolles's exuberant confessions to the Brothers Dumaine. Parolles declares that Bertram is a coward, liar, and promiscuous to boot. Bertram is forced to accept that Parolles has been duplicitous. After the wars are over, Bertram returns to Rossillion. He thinks Helena is dead and that he has slept with Diana; in fact, he is adamant about it when Diana appears before him and the king. When the bed-trick is revealed and Helena appears, ostensibly pregnant with his child and bearing his ring, he happily concedes defeat. She has fulfilled the requirements he stipulated in his letter as being necessary for him to accept her as his wife, and he vows to love her forever.

Commentators are divided over Bertram. Most agree that he is immature and full of shortcomings, but some critics find him sincere and repentant by the end of the play and thus worthy of the honorable Helena. Others find this turnaround in his character implausible and false. "No Shakespearean hero is so degraded and so unsparingly presented," wrote Russell Fraser in the New Cambridge edition of the play. One of the harshest summaries of Bertram's character came from renowned literary critic and philosopher Samuel Johnson, who summarized Bertram (as quoted in Fraser) as "a man noble without generosity, and young without truth; who marries Helena as a coward and leaves her as a profligate; when she is dead by his unkindness, sneaks home to a second marriage, is accused by a woman whom he has wronged, defends himself by falsehood, and is dismissed to happiness." The outrage, for those who dislike Bertram, is that he is given a happy ending he does not deserve.

Critics who argue that Bertram has truly repented by the end of the play suggest that it is his immaturity and desire for life experience that cause him to initially reject Helena. Elizabethan audiences, they argue, would have found Bertram's desire to go to war entirely honorable. Likewise, his blindness to Parolles's true nature is attributed to his inexperience, but once it is demonstrated via the kidnapping episode, Bertram becomes wiser. Those scholars who find Bertram entirely despicable and without merit conclude that his acceptance of Helena in the final scene of the play is one calculated to save his neck, as he finds himself backed into a corner with all the evidence (Helena, Diana, and Parolles all testify against him) stacked against him. A few critics abstain from roundly praising or condemning Bertram, offering other ways to interpret his character.

Brothers Dumaine

The Brothers Dumaine, sometimes called the two French lords, serve as captains for the Duke of Florence in the war with Sienna. They are honorable men, fond of Helena, friends with Bertram, and convinced of Parolles's bad nature from the start. They try in vain to convince Bertram that Parolles cannot be trusted. In order to prove their case, the Brothers Dumaine enact a plan to ambush Parolles and reveal his true nature to Bertram. They disguise themselves as enemy soldiers and kidnap Parolles near Florence when Parolles embarks on a mock-heroic quest to recapture the regiment's drum. The Brothers pretend to speak a different language, and while Parolles is blindfolded, he betrays Bertram openly and vociferously.

Countess of Rossillion

The Countess of Rossillion is Bertram's mother, and she is still mourning the recent death of her husband. She has also willingly become Helena's guardian since the young woman's father, a physician of local renown, has also recently passed away. Kind and generous, the countess exemplifies the best of the noble tradition and encourages Helena's love for Bertram, even though she thinks her son is foolish and headstrong for rejecting the talented, vivacious girl. The countess rates honesty and virtue higher than valor in battle or nobility of rank, even when this means that she must side against Bertram. She believes her son is old enough to get married, but too young to go into battle. She mourns Bertram's departure for Paris in the same way she mourns the loss of her husband.

The countess's fondness for Helena is evident when she tells the girl she loves her as if she were her own daughter. But when Helena offers to travel to Paris to heal the king, the countess encourages her to go. Even after Helena professes her love for the countess's son, the countess is understanding and does not discourage Helena's passion. She understands the spell of "love's strong passion," having fallen under it herself when she was younger.

The countess has been widely praised as one of Shakespeare's best female characters. Famed nineteenth-century critic and playwright George Bernard Shaw (as quoted in Fraser) called the countess "the most beautiful old woman's part ever written." One of the most famous actresses to play the role was Academy Award-winner Judi Dench, who played the countess in 2003 at the Swan Theatre in Stratford, England.

Diana

The daughter of the Widow Capilet, Diana is courted by the Count of Rossillion while he is fighting with the king's regiment in Florence. She is a virgin, and she knows Bertram's reputation as a cad, and that he is married. When Helena arrives in Florence as a traveler and agrees to stay at the Widow's inn, Diana tells her about the count's awful wife. At first, Helena pretends to be someone else, but after she confesses to being Bertram's wife,

Diana agrees to the bed-trick scheme as a way to preserve her own honor. She is also happy to help Helena achieve the demands of Bertram's letter. After the bed-trick has been carried out successfully, she and her mother accompany Helena back to Paris.

Diana plays a major role in revealing the bed-trick in the play's final act. She delights in this role, presenting a maddening riddle for the king, Bertram, and others to decipher. She insists she never slept with Bertram, even as Bertram insists that she did. When the king threatens to put her in jail for her insolence, she presents her bail in the form of Helena, the answer to the riddle and the person they all thought was dead. When all is revealed, the king applauds Diana's role in the bed-trick scheme and rewards her by letting her choose a husband from among the men at court. She will thus be spared the hardship and poverty of her life in Florence. For her, the story truly ends well.

Duke of Florence

The Duke of Florence welcomes Bertram and Parolles when they escape Paris to fight the war. He is allied with France in a war against Sienna, another province of what would later become Italy.

Helena

Helena is the daughter of the recently deceased court physician, Gerard de Narbon, from whom she has learned his healing secrets. She has become the ward of the Countess of Rossillion, with whom she has a very maternal relationship, though she has fallen in love with the countess's son, Bertram. She is disturbed by the thought of being considered the countess's daughter, because that would make Bertram her brother and her romantic interest in him would be unseemly. Because of these concerns, she admits her love for Bertram to the countess, who is sympathetic to the girl's predicament. Helena is admired by nearly everyone except Bertram for her charm, beauty, intelligence, and honesty. Her name, as several characters in the play remind her, is equivocal with Helen of Troy, the most beautiful woman of Ancient Greece, over whom the Trojan War was fought.

Helena is tormented by the thought of being separated from Bertram when he departs for Paris. She takes it upon herself, with the countess's blessing, to travel to Paris in order to heal the king, who is suffering from an incurable condition, but also because it will keep her in proximity to Bertram. She miraculously heals the king and thereby earns his loyalty, admiration, and a valuable ring that figures prominently in the story when the bed-trick is revealed.

Bertram rejects Helena because of her lowborn status. He is a count, and she is a commoner. No matter how virtuous she may be, it would be improper to marry her. Helena understands this, yet she does not accept it. She takes matters into her own hands and hatches a plan: first, to become

Bertram's wife, and second, to fulfill his demands to obtain his ring and bear his child. Even in the face of repeated rejection, she persists in her goals, so strong is her infatuation with Bertram.

Helena has the gift of healing, as did her father, and bets the king her life that she can make him well, another example of her remarkable self-confidence. He accepts the offer, and as a favor in return, Helena asks for Bertram's hand in marriage. The king readily complies.

Helena is considered the central figure in the play, and all of the major themes of the play (gender issues, desire, the bed-trick, marriage, and social class) are influenced by her actions. As the heroine of *All's Well That Ends Well*, Helena is often described by admiring commentators as noble, virtuous, honorable, and regenerative, and by detractors as obsessive and narrow-minded. Her dogged pursuit of Bertram has been both ridiculed (particularly in Victorian times) as unfeminine and commended as being bold, mostly in more recent times. Many wonder why she is attracted to a man who does not like her at all. Nearly all critics agree that she is a complex character.

Fraser and others find similarities between Helena and the real-life historical figure Christine de Pisan, an educated woman of the early fifteenth century who was renowned for her piety, goodness, intelligence, and a type of proto-feminism in which she attributed a woman's success to her own resourcefulness. Additionally, her father was the well-known doctor and astrologer Thomas of

Pisano, who had been called upon in 1365 to heal England's Charles V. Fraser theorizes that Shakespeare added dimension to the character of Helena by making her a knowingly frail character, as evidenced by her pilgrimage to Saint Jacques le Grand. This suggests that though Helena is strong and brave enough to get what she wants (Bertram), she understands her limitations as a person, and possibly her faults (that is, desiring the flawed Bertram is perhaps not the healthiest thing for her). "Shakespeare's Helena is frail in that 'we are all frail,'" Fraser writes, "and it is this generic human frailty that dictates the pilgrimage to Saint Jacques." Irish playwright W. B. Yeats, quoted by Patrick Carnegy in the *Spectator*, called Helena "one of Shakespeare's 'glorious women who select dreadful or empty men.'"

Commentators who unequivocally admire Helena find her guiltless in plotting to wed Bertram and in fulfilling the terms of his letter through the bed-trick. One critic even refers to her as a genius. Scholars who are critical of her character find her obsessed by her sexual passion and an example of noble womanhood degraded, using her abilities as a huntress to realize her plans for a union with Bertram with no thought of their consequences to others (primarily Diana).

Most critics, however, see Helena as a many-sided character. Several critics have noted her regenerative and restorative powers; she saves the king from almost certain death, but how she does it remains a mystery. She is the key to restoring a kingdom whose noble elders are dying and who have no honorable replacements. When Helena heals the king, she restores the kingdom at least for a time, and saves Bertram (and Diana) from making what would have been a mistake of lifelong regret. She is pregnant at the end of the play, symbolically the provider of a new generation of nobility. Other critics have noted her embodiment of both feminine passivity and masculine action. She is the desiring subject (the pursuer of Bertram), yet she longs to be the desired object (pursued by Bertram).

King of France

The King of France represents a dying breed of nobility, one in which honor and virtue are supremely important. When the play opens, he is suffering from a debilitating illness, fistula, in which some of his internal organs have developed abscesses. He is nostalgic for the past and has fond memories of Bertram's father, the former Count of Rossillion. Helena, who has followed Bertram to Paris, offers to heal the king. When she succeeds, the king is grateful and generous, giving her a valuable ring, allowing her to choose a husband from among his noblemen. When Bertram rejects Helena for being common, the king offers her a title and a dowry.

The king forbids Bertram from traveling to Florence to fight in the war, stating that the count is too young. He is protective of his troops and makes sure they are trained sufficiently. He is ambivalent about Florence's war with Sienna and allows his men to choose which side they will fight for. When the bed-trick is revealed at the play's conclusion, the king is pleased that all has worked out, and he allows Diana to choose a husband. This gesture shows that, although he is grateful and gives generous rewards, he has not learned his lesson. He offered Helena the same reward, which led to the chain of events that caused Diana to be there in the first place. However, the king's actions most likely rescue Diana (and her mother) from a life of poverty, proving he is much more forgiving of class differences than Bertram, despite possessing the ultimate title. His actions prove him to be cautious, thoughtful, and ultimately benevolent.

Lafew

Lafew is an elderly lord, a friend and confidant of the countess. He is quick to perceive the true character of Parolles, calls him a knave (an unscrupulous person), ridicules his flashy clothes, and warns Bertram against him. Lafew travels to Paris with Bertram, and he is one of Helena's strongest defenders. When the king allows her to choose a husband, he wishes he were young enough to be considered. Even though Lafew represents the old guard—he would have been close to Bertram's father—and his values are somewhat traditional, he is still a good judge of character and is capable of forgiveness. His sympathy and kindness become apparent at the end of the play when he assures the unmasked and humiliated Parolles that he will not be tossed out of the palace.

Lavatch

Lavatch is a cantankerous, pessimistic clown and servant of the Countess of Rossillion. He provides some comic relief in the play, usually in somewhat lascivious prose that espouses his gloomy world view. He is the lowest character on the totem pole in the play, so unscrupulous that even Parolles calls him a knave. He has an affair with Isabel, a servant, and gets her pregnant. He decides to marry her, but later changes his mind. Lavatch is the one older character in the play who is unwise, proving that age and wisdom do not always go together.

Parolles

Mentor and confidant to Bertram, Parolles is a social climber and a scoundrel. On the other hand, he exhibits more self-awareness than Bertram and speaks several languages. He dresses in flashy clothes that border on the ridiculous and does not put his intelligence to good use. He is a prime example of a *miles gloriosus*, a boastful soldier, which was a stock character type in Shakespeare's day. He also has qualities of a *servus callidus*, a tricky slave, another type of stock character. The first glimpse of his false allegiance to Bertram is when he tells Lafew that Bertram is not his master; he answers only to God. This displays his arrogance and disloyalty; Parolles is in service to the Count of Rossillion, and likewise is expected to remain steadfast, especially so when he follows Bertram into battle. But he betrays Bertram in Florence when he is captured and tricked into believing he is about to be tortured. His boasts and deceit finally bring about his unmasking, at last enlightening Bertram as to his true character. Parolles is quick to realize he has been a fool, suffers humiliation, and assumes a new veneer of humbleness in accepting Lafew's mercy, which will enable him to remain in Rossillion.

Parolles has a long conversation with Helena in the first act. They discuss her virginity in rather flirtatious terms. One wonders why Helena would choose to confide in Parolles, a man whose advice she would almost certainly never take. For his part, Parolles tells Helena that virginity is a handicap. The longer she preserves it, the more danger she is in of becoming damaged goods. That Parolles would give such advice to a young woman so highly regarded by the countess speaks of his contempt for those in authority as well as his lax morals.

Critics praise Shakespeare for his creation of Parolles, a character not found in Boccaccio's version of the tale, whether they like him or not. He appears in thirteen of the play's twenty-three scenes, and some consider the scene of his unmasking (the longest scene in the play) to be the structural center of the play (especially since the critical scene of the bed-trick occurs offstage). Parolles is responsible for most of the laughter (albeit scant) in the play, and although he is generally regarded as a liar, a coward, a fop, and a character lacking in honor and principle, he is essential to the plot.

For many, Parolles is a more interesting character than Bertram. Some directors have created versions of the play that revolve more around Parolles than Helena, and some renowned actors have been attracted to the part, most notably Laurence Olivier in a 1927 production. Some critics debate whether or not Parolles is a bad influence on Bertram, or if they are simply like minds that have found each other. Fraser believes that "Parolles is an extension of Bertram."

Widow Capilet

The Widow Capilet is Diana's mother, and she runs the inn in Florence where Helena stays on her pilgrimage to Saint Jacques le Grand. She tells Helena that Bertram has been trying to seduce Diana. When Helena proposes the bed-trick as a way to fulfill her wifely duties and save Diana's virginity in the process, the Widow reluctantly agrees because she sympathizes with Helena's predicament. Afterward, she accompanies Diana and Helena back to Rossillion at the end of the play. When Diana presents the bed-trick to the king and others, the Widow is excused to fetch Diana's bail, which is revealed to be Helena herself.

Gender Roles

Much of the plot of *All's Well That Ends Well* hinges on Helena's willingness to dismiss the constraints of her traditional, feminine gender role. Because Helena subverts her own prescribed gender role (mainly, that a woman should be demure and not exhibit unprompted sexual interest in a man) in pursuing her heart's desire, Bertram is also forced against his will into a reversed gender role by becoming the pursued. Her other actions are also quite bold for a woman. She engages in a frank discussion about her virginity with Parolles but is adamant about remaining a virgin, thereby embodying both gender roles of participating in a sexual debate with a man while remaining chaste. She travels alone to Paris, heals the king (traditionally a male job), and thereby is allowed to choose her husband, a complete subversion of normal gender roles. She also leaves Rossillion and travels on a very long pilgrimage all by herself, arranges the bed-trick for her own benefit, and craftily stages her own death in order to get what she wants. However, also implicit in her proactive role is a desire to engage in a more traditional role. She longs to be desired by Bertram and to have his child. In the sense that both of these happen at the end of the play, all does end well for Helena.

This dual nature of Helena's character, in which she exhibits elements of both female passiveness and masculine action, is demonstrated in the scene where she selects Bertram as a husband. She emphasizes her low social status to the king and how unworthy she is. It could be that she is only playing up her feminine side in order to seem more attractive to the assembled suitors. But when Bertram rejects and humiliates her in front of the entire court, she retracts her choice. The marriage proceeds only because the king insists on keeping his word. When Bertram leaves her—their marriage still unconsummated—to go to the wars in Italy, she passively sits at home and then wanders off as a pilgrim so that Bertram can return to Rossillion. In a sense, this is a passive act in that it reveals her sense of defeat. Even when Bertram sends the letter with the conditions of his acceptance of her as his wife, conditions that he believes she could never fulfill, Helena is not angered but takes pity on him instead, noting how she stole rank by marrying him. Finally, once Helena has completed the tasks Bertram required of her and he takes her as his wife, she is satisfied with the role of wife and mother, which will presumably place her permanently back in a more traditional female role.

Several critics note the quest-romance and the knight-errant themes in *All's Well That Ends Well*, only in this case the initiator of action—the hero— is a woman. Helena possesses the knowledge and skill to influence events and other characters and thus is able to secure Bertram as a husband.

However, she cannot force him to love her, and his rejection requires her to pursue an alternate plan of action. Some think that Helena's active role, her ability to go out and get what she wants (Bertram), is motivated only by sexual desire. Others excuse her unorthodox means of fulfilling Bertram's conditions because they were created with the intent of being impossible to fulfill. Thus, she had no other recourse after having been publicly humiliated by Bertram than to arrange the bed-trick.

Bed-trick/Marriage

The bed-trick in *All's Well That Ends Well* pervades much of the commentary on the play and intersects with the discussion of marriage. Commentators tend to focus on whether Helena's use of the bed-trick is justified and lawful and whether it provides a means for a satisfactory ending to the play. Critics who believe Helena's switch with Diana is justified argue that as Bertram's wife, Helena had every right to take Diana's place and consummate her marriage, thus saving both Diana and Bertram from dishonor. Helena saves a maiden from what would have been a grave mistake, and she keeps Bertram from committing what would have been an unlawful act of adultery. By thus saving Bertram, and, as a result, securing his ring and carrying his child, Helena is an agent in restoring the dying kingdom. Those who find Helena's actions unlawful note that Helena is actually encouraging Bertram to engage in adultery (even though Helena knows that what she is doing is technically lawful). They note that although Helena satisfactorily fulfills Bertram's requirements in his letter, this does not necessarily dictate a happy ending, since their sexual union was based on deception.

Social Class

Despite the fact that she lives in the palace, Helena is a commoner. Her mother died when she was young, and her father was a doctor. Without property, money, or a title to her name, she has no assets to attract Bertram, who is a member of the noble class. Most marriages in that time were arranged to benefit both families, and Bertram's marriage to Helena would benefit only her. Some view this as a justifiable reason for Bertram to reject Helena. However, we are told early on in the play that Helena possesses true nobility and honor, which cannot be obtained by birth. Bertram, though born with wealth and status, has no nobility or honor to speak of. The noble and honorable older generation, represented by the king, the countess, and Lafew, recognize Helena's virtues and Bertram's lack of them.

A few commentators have noted that wealth and rank actually mean little to either Helena or Bertram. Helena wants Bertram, not his money, and Bertram wants his freedom, not a marriage to a woman everyone considers noble and virtuous. If Bertram were truly in pursuit of great rank, he would have accepted Helena, whom the king has endowed with wealth to make her Bertram's equal (although a few critics note that this is actually unnecessary, for Helena's fine qualities erase the social gap between her and Bertram). Also, if Bertram were truly invested in maintaining his class distinction, he would not have befriended Parolles, a man of notably low birth and, worse, base and vile qualities.

Youth versus Experience

The bittersweet tone of *All's Well That Ends Well* is established by the play's older characters, especially the Countess of Rossillion and Lafew, both of whom have suffered the loss of loved ones and express their patience with those of the younger generation. The countess sympathizes with Helena's passion for Bertram, because she was once young and in love herself. Likewise, Lafew forgives Parolles for being a traitor and gives him a second chance by offering him a position. The King of France offers his sympathy to Bertram on the loss of his father, and tells the count he is too young to fight in the war. Ultimately, the happy ending of the play is in the fact that the elders will take no retribution out on the younger generation for the follies to which they have subjected themselves. A counterpoint to this is Lavatch, the aging clown, who talks dirty, impregnates a chambermaid, and then changes his mind about marrying her. He still acts like a child, and his position as a clown—a person no one takes seriously—underscores that fact. Lavatch exhibits the whims of a young person, even though he is old. He serves as an example of the misery that awaits those who fail to live up to their responsibilities as they enter into adulthood. The older generation understands that youth is a time of trial and error, and they remain hopeful that the younger generation—Bertram and Parolles especially—have learned their lessons as their elders continue to take them under their wings and prepare them for the future.

Endings

The abrupt ending of *All's Well That Ends Well* is partly responsible for giving the play its problem status. Does the play end well? If so, for whom? Most modern critics conclude that the ending is unsatisfactory and unconvincing, even though it provides the required comedic resolution whereby the hero and heroine are joined at last. They have a hard time believing that Bertram could enter into a happy marriage with Helena after being confronted with her deception. Early commentators, however, tended to have less trouble accepting the ending and argued that Elizabethan audiences, familiar with the folk tales on which the play was based, would not have found the ending lacking.

Some argue that Shakespeare lost interest in the character of Helena once she succeeded in securing Bertram, and he proceeded to a hasty closing scene. Others sense a difficult future ahead for Helena and Bertram because, even though he now acknowledges Helena as his wife, he has demonstrated no change of heart through his actions. Marjorie Garber, in her book *Shakespeare After All*, approves of the ending because of the careful way it was set up. The ending "is constructed like an elaborate mechanism and goes off with a bang in the powerful final scene." Furthermore, she states, that "whatever our estimation of the callow but promising Bertram and the astonishingly patient Helena, both the genre of fairy tale and the history of noble marriage suggest that ending well—at least onstage—may be the best medicine."

Topics for Further Study

- Helena is Shakespeare's only female character to address the audience through a soliloquy. Scan her soliloquy in act 1, scene 1, that begins "O, were that all." Do you find any particular meter or rhyme scheme? Do you agree with critics who say that the prose of *All's Well That Ends Well* is sloppy and uninspired? List three reasons why it is so or why it is not so.

- Using a map, trace the path from Rossillion in France to Galicia in Spain, where the Cathedral of Santiago is. Where is Florence in relation to the cathedral? Calculate the distance between Rossillion and Florence. How long do you think it took Helena to get there on foot? Discuss the weather, terrain, and other obstacles (natural or man-made) she may have encountered on her journey.

- Lafew chides Parolles for his flashy clothes, asking, "Pray you, sir, who's his tailor?" and describing him to the countess as that "snipped-taffeta fellow there, whose villainous saffron would have made all the unbaked and doughy youth of a nation in his colour." Research clothing of the Elizabethan period and photocopy or draw three examples of the types of outfits Parolles may have been wearing, befitting his social class and garish taste, that Lafew was making fun of.

- Some critics have noted the

discrepancy between the rash behavior of the play's younger characters (namely, Bertram, Parolles, and Helena), and the forgiving nature of the play's older characters (Lafew, the countess, and the king). Using the theory of personality developed by twentieth-century German psychologist Erik Erikson, who described the eight stages of psychosocial development, write a five hundred word essay explaining how the characters' stages of development influence their behavior. Support your reasoning with examples.

Style

New Comedy

In literature, "comedy" refers to a story with a happy ending and a "tragedy" is a story with a sad ending. The earliest comedies date from fifth century B.C.E. Greece, and that style is known as Old Comedy, which was known for lampooning famous people and events of the day. Beginning in 320 B.C.E., the style of comedy changed to reflect stock characters and situations. This style was dubbed New Comedy, and often featured a love story of a young couple as part of the plot. Some other famous New Comedies include Dante's *Divine Comedy* and Geoffrey Chaucer's *The Canterbury Tales. All's Well That Ends Well* is also a New Comedy. When Bertram is confronted with evidence of his shenanigans and Helena outwits him in fulfilling his impossible demands, he undergoes a complete change of heart. Helena obtains her prize—Bertram. Diana is also saved from a meager existence, the king's life is saved, the countess gains a daughter, and even Parolles repents. Everyone is better off than when the play began, and the solemn tone of mourning has been replaced by wedding bells and the good news of Helena's pregnancy. Parolles exhibits traits of both a *miles gloriosus* (boastful soldier) and a *servus callidus* (tricky slave), which are both stock characters of New Comedy. There are, however, plot elements responsible for the play's reputation as a problem play, which are those that run counter to the idea of comedy. These include the feeling of foreboding caused by Bertram's superficial acceptance of Helena, and the king's offer to Diana to choose a husband, which one suspects could create a whole new set of problems.

Double Entendre

A double entendre is a word or phrase that can be construed as having two meanings, due to an intentional ambiguity on the part of the author or speaker. Often, one of those meanings is risqué. Much of the humor in Shakespeare's plays comes from double entendres, and in *All's Well That Ends Well* the speech of Lavatch, the clown, and words of Parolles and others can be construed as double entendres. For example, when Helena asks Parolles for advice on how to retain her virginity, he replies that it is impossible: "Man, setting down before you, will undermine you and blow you up." To which Helena responds, "Bless our poor virginity from under-miners and blowers-up! Is there no military policy how virgins might blow up men?" The humor in their exchange comes from the double meaning of the term "blow you up." Undoubtedly, Helena is clever enough to understand the significance of what she is saying to Parolles, and it represents her complexity as a character. She is a virtuous maiden, intent on retaining her virtue, yet she is not above engaging in a bit of ribald repartee with a man—one of low morals, at that. In another example, Lavatch tells Lafew the difference between his roles as a fool and a knave. He says he is "a fool, sir, at a woman's service, and a knave at a man's." When Lafew asks what the difference is, Lavatch responds, "I would cozen the man of his wife and do his service." In this case, the term "service" means he would take up the duties of being the wife's husband, including those of a sexual nature.

Aphorism

An aphorism is a concise and memorable phrase that lends itself to being quoted outside of its original context. "All's well that ends well" itself is an aphorism—one that was known to audiences at the time Shakespeare wrote his play. Though *All's Well That Ends Well* does not contain as many well-known aphorisms as some of his other plays, such as "To be, or not to be, that is the question" from *Hamlet* or "Out, out, damn spot" from *Macbeth*, it has its moments. In particular is Helena's declaration that "Our remedies oft in ourselves do lie, / Which we ascribe to heaven." She means that when a person prays for the answer to a problem and it is solved, it is likely that the person solved the problem him or herself. God did not solve it for them. She uses this belief to pursue Bertram after he leaves for Paris; she knows that if she is ever to win his love it will be through her own actions, not simply by wishing or praying. Another aphorism is Parolles's declaration that "a young man married is a man that's marred," when he sympathizes with

Bertram's plight of being married to Helena against his will. Diana's friend Mariana warns her against Bertram's advances, stating, "no legacy is so rich as honesty," meaning that the greatest thing she has going for herself is her virtue, and to lose it to Bertram would be tragic. All of these phrases can stand alone in meaning beyond the context of the play.

Literature in Shakespeare's Time

Shakespeare based much of *All's Well That Ends Well* on Giovanni Boccaccio's *Decameron*, a collection of one hundred novellas wrapped around a frame story. Boccaccio was a Florentine writer of the fourteenth century who wrote in the Italian vernacular, thereby making the *Decameron* popular among the middle class, as opposed to scholars who shunned anything not written in Latin. The *Decameron*, which means literally "ten days," is ostensibly the tale of ten people (seven women and three men), who are hiding out in the hills above the city of Florence during an outbreak of the Black Plague. Each day, they take turns telling stories in order to pass the time. Many of their stories are retellings of folk tales.

Boccaccio's *Decameron* influenced many writers, beginning with Geoffrey Chaucer, also a fourteenth-century writer, who adopted some of the Italian writer's ideas for *The Canterbury Tales*, which is commonly acknowledged as the first work of poetry written in English. *The Canterbury Tales* adopts a similar frame story; an assembled group of pilgrims takes turns telling each other stories on a sojourn from London to Canterbury.

Even if Shakespeare was not directly influenced by the *Decameron*, he almost certainly was familiar with *The Palace of Pleasure*, a work by William Painter closely based on the *Decameron*. Painter's thirty-eighth story in the collection is about Giletta di Narbona, the daughter of a physician who cures the King of France. In return, she asks the king if she can marry Beltramo, the Count of Rossiglione. Though the king complies, the count escapes to Florence. Giletta follows him, seduces him against his knowledge, and becomes pregnant with twin boys. When the scheme is revealed, the count promptly apologizes and becomes a willfully faithful husband. In Shakespeare's telling, he added the characters of Parolles, the countess, and Lafew in order to give the story more depth.

Many critics have surmised that Shakespeare based the character of Helena on Christine de Pizan, an early-fifteenth-century writer who was the daughter of the famous Venetian physician and astronomer Tommaso di Benvenuto da Pizzano. De Pizan was the first widely known female writer, well-regarded, who exhibits many of the admirable traits with which Shakespeare endowed Helena. Her *Book of the City of Ladies* is widely regarded as a proto-feminist masterpiece.

Traditions of Marriage

In Shakespeare's time, marriages were usually arranged. A love match was unusual, and even more unusual was a woman choosing her prospective groom. Bertram's objection to marrying Helena is rooted in these traditions. Because he is a count, he would have expected to marry someone of a similar status, not a commoner with neither wealth nor property to her name. A man would base his opinion of his prospective wife on the extent of her dowry, or marriage portion, which would include any land, money, or other goods, such as jewelry, which would become the husband's property upon marriage (as would his wife). Helena had none of these, so Bertram considered her an inappropriate wife, regardless of her talents and personality.

As for the marriage ceremony, the king in *All's Well That Ends Well* dispenses with tradition, which would have necessitated the Crying of the Banns, a public declaration of the couple's intent to marry on three successive Sundays in their respective churches. This procedure allowed people time to voice objections to the marriage, for whatever reason. Exceptions to the Crying of the Banns were rare; ironically, Shakespeare himself was one of these exceptions, due to the fact that his prospective wife, Ann Hathaway, was already pregnant. As in *All's Well That Ends Well*, certainly the king had the power to conduct a wedding ceremony without a prior Crying of the Banns.

Other traditions alluded to in the play include the expectation that the bride be a virgin. The bed-trick did indeed save Diana from ruining her life. Additionally, an exchange of rings was not uncommon, but it was not the norm. When Bertram states that Helena would never wear his ring, this would have been widely understood to mean that his ring on her finger would symbolize his acceptance of their union. Likewise, when Helena tricks Bertram into wearing her ring (the one the king gave her), she has succeeded in claiming him as would a bride who presented her groom with a wedding ring.

Medicine and Healing

In Shakespeare's time, medicine was little more than trial and error mixed with a great deal of superstition. Little was known about proven treatments, and disease and germs were not understood. Sanitation and hygiene, even among the upper classes, was rudimentary at best. Streets were filled with garbage and raw sewage, which spilled over into the rivers and lakes. Rats and vermin abounded, and no one made the connection between these conditions and the sicknesses that killed people. Typhoid, syphilis, influenza, and plague exacted a toll on life expectancy, as did poor nutrition, which led to life-threatening anemia and dysentery. Many upper-class women covered their faces with white make-up, which contained high amounts of lead. The make-up poisoned, and even killed, many of them.

Because these health dangers were not understood, the work of physicians often included astrology. Astrologers and doctors, such as Tommaso de Benvenuto da Pizzano (Shakespeare's possible model for Helena's father, Gerard de Narbon), often resorted to bleeding people when they became ill in an effort to cleanse their bodies from bad humors, or bodily fluids.

Physicians in Shakespeare's day wore unusual outfits, complete with a long black cloak, leather gloves, leather boots, a pointed hood, and a mask with a long, pointed beak, which was filled with bergamot oil. Though the outfit may have been rooted in superstition, it probably did protect doctors, simply because it provided a barrier against the germs and bugs that would have covered their patients. Their odd appearance, however, often inspired dread in townspeople, who came to regard physicians with wariness. Anyway, only the very wealthy—mainly the nobles—would have been able to afford treatment by a doctor. Other segments of the population might be treated by a barber, who, in addition to cutting hair, also pulled teeth and bled patients.

The ailment the King of France suffers from in *All's Well That Ends Well*, fistula, which is an abscess that creates an opening between two organs, would not have been well understood at the time, and it is true that a physician may have told those afflicted with the condition that there was nothing that could be done. How Helena cures the king so quickly and completely is inexplicable, certainly in terms of medical knowledge either then or now, and her healing powers remain one of the story's most implausible folk-tale elements.

Pilgrimages

After she heals the king and is wed to Bertram, Helena is ordered back to Rossillion. Distraught by Bertram's letter stating he will never return home as long as she is there, she departs on a pilgrimage to the burial site of Saint Jacques le Grande. Also known as the Way of St. James, the pilgrimage leads travelers to the Cathedral of Santiago in northwest Spain, the burial site of the Apostle James, St. James the Greater, a follower of Jesus Christ and the brother of the Apostle John. The purpose of the pilgrimage was to have the pilgrim's greatest sins forgiven; the only other two pilgrimages that could do the same thing were to Rome and Jerusalem. There were several popular routes pilgrims could take to the shrine, each passing through other towns and stopping at notable locations along the way. A majority of those who undertook the trip were French, and the Way includes many stops in France before continuing on to Spain. The Cathedral of Santiago is still a popular pilgrimage site in the twenty-first century, and priests hold weekly services to welcome those who have made the trip, often on foot or bicycle.

In Shakespeare's time, this pilgrimage was still popular but considered somewhat dangerous because of the violence resulting from the Protestant Reformation. Audiences would have been familiar with the journey and accepted Helena's reasons for undertaking it. However, given that Helena leaves for the trip from Rossillion, which borders Spain, how she ends up in Florence, which is hundreds of miles in the opposite direction from the shrine, is never explained. The fact that she is traveling alone is also puzzling.

Compare & Contrast

- **1600:** Rossillion (Rousillon in French) is a Spanish territory, formerly part of the Kingdom of Majorca. It is conquered by Louis XIII in 1642 and is ceded to France by the Treaty of the Pyrenees in 1659.

  Today: Rousillon is a thriving region in France that produces vast quantities of wine, particularly red *vin ordinaire*. The area and its capital city, Perpignan, is a major tourist region.

- **1600:** Doctors can do little to cure fistula, a medical ailment in which two organs become connected via the abnormal development of an abscess or passageway. Typical treatment may include bleeding with leeches.

  Today: Treatment for fistula includes a surgical procedure known as a fistulotomy, followed by antibiotics. Doctors prevent recurrence of the condition by treating other conditions that sometimes cause fistula, such as Crohn's disease and colitis.

- **1600:** Christians from around Europe, but particularly from France, undertake the pilgrimage known as the Way of St. James, which leads them to the Cathedral of Santiago in the north of Spain. It is an arduous journey undertaken on foot or by horse, and may take many months. Hostels are located along the way to provide accommodations for the travelers. The pilgrimage was sometimes undertaken as penance for a grave crime.

Today: Thousands of pilgrims travel on foot or by bike each year to the Cathedral of Santiago along the pilgrimage route, which was named a UNESCO World Heritage Site in 1993. Pilgrims receive an official pass that allows them to stay in hostels at reduced rates along the way.

Critical interpretation of *All's Well That Ends Well* often hinges on whether the critic believes the play lives up to its title. The widespread belief that it does not has led to its reputation as a problem play, or rather, a comedy with strings attached. Shakespeare, who was by all accounts an astute observer of the human condition, seems not to have invested the lead characters of Bertram and Helena with enough depth to understand the error of their ways, or permitted them to have meaningful moments of enlightenment that would bring about the necessary changes. For centuries, critics have been vexed by Bertram's about-face in the last scene, when he suddenly realizes his foolishness and agrees to be Helena's faithful husband and the father of their child. At the very least, critics have detected a bit of irony in the title; even Shakespeare had to know that these characters were not about to live happily ever after. As they settled into their marriage, would the very pro-active Helena have been satisfied to revert to the feminine ideal of a passive wife? And would Bertram truly be able to put his days as a scoundrel behind him and love a woman who previously repulsed him? How can their relationship succeed, given that it is based upon the deception of the bed-trick? All of these questions pose problems for critics. Some find ways to reconcile them with Shakespeare's intentions, and others cannot. For them, *All's Well That Ends Well* is one of Shakespeare's sloppier plays, and therefore unsuccessful. As William Witherle Lawrence writes in *Shakespeare's Problem Comedies*, "critical explanations have nowhere shown wider divergence than in regard to this play, nor have the points at issue ever been more sharply marked."

The play has been praised for several factors, however, including the characterization of the Countess of Rossillion, one of Shakespeare's more well-rounded older females. In fact, most of the older characters in the play exhibit good judgment and work hard at guiding the younger generation into accepting their roles and responsibilities. Russell Fraser, in his introduction to *All's Well That Ends Well*, published in the New Cambridge Shakespeare series, goes so far as to say "*All's Well That Ends Well* is a great play whose time has come round." In support of this idea, he writes that,

> [Shakespeare's] characters may change for the better or worse, and things beginning at the worst may turn upwards in the course of the play. But no character puts off altogether what he was at first, and if the play begins in darkness, the darkness is never altogether dispelled. Characters in *All's Well* are left open to mortality, and in the world they inhabit the best is behind. This feeling, conveyed in the first scene of the play, is borne out in the ending.

In a similar manner, Eileen Z. Cohen, writing in *Philological Quarterly*, defends Shakespeare's use of the bed-trick as a narrative device and disagrees with those who find it unbecoming of Helena. "[Shakespeare] requires us to believe that virtuous maidens can initiate and participate in the bed-trick. He insists that it saves lives and nurtures marriage, that it leads the duped men out of ignorance and toward understanding, and that the women who orchestrate it end with a clearer image of themselves."

Most critics also approve of the way Shakespeare fleshed out Boccaccio's original story, "Giletta of Narbonne," by adding the subplot of Parolles, in which the kidnapping trick serves as a parallel to the bed-trick and exposes his treasonous behavior to Bertram. In addition to fulfilling the New Comedy roles of the *miles gloriosus* and the *servus callidus*, Parolles, in the scene of his unmasking, serves as the fulcrum of the play, since the other main event—the bed-trick itself—takes place off stage. According to R. J. Schork, writing in *Philological Quarterly*, "The several New Comedic roles enacted by Parolles in *All's Well That Ends Well* are proof of Shakespeare's versatility and ingenuity in blending New Comedic motifs into a plot lifted from Boccaccio. All the characters in the play ... could be matched to analogous characters in Roman comedy; none of them, however, plays the stock role straight." Others attribute the play's weaknesses to its folk-tale elements, which almost by definition render it immune to criticism based on lack of character development. According to Lawrence, both the Healing of the King and the Fulfillment of the Tasks are well-known folk-tale conventions that turn up in many cultures, including India, Norway, and Turkey, and which would have influenced Boccaccio. Many of these tales also "exalt the cleverness and devotion of the woman," Lawrence writes in *Shakespeare's Problem Comedies*, "the wits of the wife are more than a match for those of the husband, and her purpose is a happy reunion with him."

No matter what the play's virtues, critics eventually return to its problems. Irish poet W. B. Yeats, according to *Spectator* theater critic Patrick Carnegy, "saw Helena as one of Shakespeare's 'glorious women who select dreadful or empty men.'" And Samuel Johnson, says Carnegy, wrote off Bertram "as a bad lot whose fate was, in a devastating phrase, to be 'dismissed to happiness.'" However, Charles Isherwood, reviewing a modern production of the play for the *New York Times*, writes that Bertram is "an adolescent forced before his time into manhood, and is only obeying the impulses of his young blood when he flees the embrace of his wiser new wife." In another *New York Times* review of the play, Alvin Klein notes that "most contemporary directors have transposed into the twentieth century the play's very considerable obstacles, which have nothing to do with time, but with the tediousness, thinness and inherent unpleasantness of a timelessly ineffectual tale." Ultimately, according to Maurice Charney in *All of Shakespeare*, a major problem with the play is the bed-trick itself: "We are not comfortable with the fiction of substituting one woman for another, as if in bed all women were alike." Additionally, in regard to Helena's miracle cure for the king, Charney wonders "if Helena does indeed have magical powers, why does she need to go to so much trouble to fulfill her tasks?"

In the end, Helena's feminist take on creating her own reality in a patriarchal world has proven attractive enough for some to resurrect the play from its near-forgotten status of previous centuries. Modern-day directors have taken pains to show why she would be attracted to Bertram, sometimes successfully and other times less so. The play's other themes—of generational differences, class distinctions—have proven sturdy enough to sustain the play through its more questionable moments. It may remain forever a problem play, but critics have shown that it contains enough nuance, humor, and truth to remain a relevant part of Shakespeare's canon. Poet John Berryman, in his essay "Pathos and Dream" quoted in *Berryman's Shakespeare*, notes that Shakespeare wrote four plays that are deemed "failures": *The Two Gentlemen of Verona, King John, Timon of Athens*, and *All's Well That Ends Well*. "The reasons for his failure in each case were different," Berryman says, "but at least he was always capable of failure, and it is pleasant to know this."

Sources

Carnegy, Patrick, "Fruitful Follies," in the *Spectator*, Vol. 293, No. 9151, December 27, 2003, p. 42.

Charney, Maurice, "All's Well That Ends Well," in *All of Shakespeare*, Columbia University Press, 1993, pp. 95-103.

Cohen, Eileen Z., "'Virtue Is Bold': The Bed-Trick and Characterization in *All's Well That Ends Well* and *Measure for Measure*," in *Philological Quarterly*, Vol. 65, 1986, pp. 171-86.

Fraser, Russell, ed., "Introduction" to *All's Well That Ends Well*, Cambridge University Press, 1985, pp. 1-37.

Garber, Marjorie, "All's Well That Ends Well," in *Shakespeare After All*, Pantheon, 2004, pp. 617-33.

Haffenden, John, ed., "Pathos and Dream," in *Berryman's Shakespeare: Essays, Letters, and Other Writings by John Berryman*, Farrar, Straus & Giroux, 1999, p. 51.

Isherwood, Charles, "Maybe He's Just Not into You, Helena," in the *New York Times*, February 14, 2006.

Klein, Alvin, "What a Woman Wants (Never Mind Why)," in the *New York Times*, July 26, 1998.

Lawrence, William Witherle, "All's Well That Ends Well," in *Shakespeare's Problem Comedies*, 2nd ed., Frederick Ungar, 1960, pp. 32-77.

Schork, R. J., "The Many Masks of Parolles," in *Philological Quarterly*, Vol. 76, No. 3, Summer 1997, p. 263.

Shakespeare, William, *All's Well That Ends Well*, 2nd Series, edited by G. K. Hunter, Arden Shakespeare, 1968.

Further Reading

Beck, Ervin, "Shakespeare's *All's Well That Ends Well*," in *Explicator*, Vol. 55, No. 3, Spring 1997, p. 123.

> Beck writes about the symbolism of Helena's name, particularly as it relates to other characters in classical literature, all of whom were bearers of truth.

Briggs, Julia, "Shakespeare's Bed-Tricks," in *Essays in Criticism*, Vol. 44, No. 4, October 1994, pp. 293-314.

> Briggs discusses the influences on Shakespeare in his use of the bed-trick and how Shakespeare used the bed-trick in his own work. Briggs focuses on *Arcadia*, a work preceding Shakespeare's plays, and Shakespeare's own *Measure for Measure* and *All's Well That Ends Well*.

Bryant, J. A., Jr., "*All's Well That Ends Well* and *Measure for Measure*," in *Shakespeare and the Uses of Comedy*, University Press of Kentucky, 1986, pp. 203-20.

> Bryant examines how the two plays, although "traditional" comedies, veer from the usual paths of such tales,

arriving "at the prescribed destination with marks of the passage still showing."

Clark, Ira, "The Trappings of *All's Well That Ends Well*," in *Style*, Vol. 39, No. 3, Fall 2005, p. 277.

Clark focuses on the verbal trickery and the plot reversals of the play, arguing that these "traps" are essential style elements and should be analyzed as such.

Friedman, Michael D., "Male Bonds and Marriage in *All's Well and Much Ado*," in *Studies in English Literature*, Vol. 35, No. 2, Spring 1995, pp. 231-49.

Friedman discusses male bonding in *All's Well That Ends Well* and *Much Ado about Nothing*, primarily the relationship between Bertram and Parolles, and Claudio and Benedick, and how it pertains to marriage in the plays.

Haley, David, "Bertram at Court," in *Shakespeare's Courtly Mirror: Reflexivity and Prudence in All's Well That Ends Well*, University of Delaware Press, 1993, pp. 17-51.

Haley's article examines *All's Well That Ends Well* as a courtly play (and Shakespeare's approach to the courtier in general), with specific emphasis on Bertram as a courtier.

——————, "Helena's Love," in *Shakespeare's*

Courtly Mirror: Reflexivity and Prudence in All's Well That Ends Well, University of Delaware Press, 1993, pp. 87-122.

> This essay by Haley examines Helena's character, including her love melancholy, her "prophetic virtue" and "providential mission," and her "erotic motive" to be united with Bertram after he has rejected her (thus abandoning "providence for Eros").

Hodgdon, Barbara, "The Making of Virgins and Mothers: Sexual Signs, Substitute Scenes and Doubled Presences in *All's Well That Ends Well*," in *Philological Quarterly*, Vol. 66, No. 1, Winter 1987, pp. 47-71.

> Hodgdon approaches a reading of *All's Well That Ends Well* from Helena's point of view, examining in particular how Shakespeare based his play on Boccaccio's play and what he did differently; how "sexual signs are articulated in character and event"; and how substitute scenes are used, particularly the bed-trick.

Hunt, Maurice, "Words and Deeds in *All's Well That Ends Well*," in *Modern Language Quarterly*, Vol. 48, No. 4, December 1987, pp. 320-38.

> Hunt's essay examines the "competition" between words and deeds in *All's Well That Ends Well*

primarily through the King of France, who vacillates between valuing word and deed and thus the two cannot be brought into harmony; Helena, through whom Shakespeare implies that "not only that deeds can on occasion speak but also that they can prompt an eventual honesty in words"; and Bertram, who merges word and deed in the final scenes of the play when he embraces Helena.

Jardine, Lisa, "Cultural Confusion and Shakespeare's Learned Heroines: 'These Are Old Paradoxes,'" in *Shakespeare Quarterly*, Vol. 38, No. 1, Spring 1987, pp. 1-18.

Jardine's article discusses how Helena and Portia, in, respectively, *All's Well That Ends Well* and *The Merchant of Venice*, possessed knowledge traditionally associated with the "male sphere." Helena, in particular possessed knowledge as a healer (the community's "wise woman"), in her upbringing (her "education"), and as the "woman who knows" in her deception of Bertram. Jardine discusses the tension between possessing knowledge as a part of female virtue and possessing it in the "male sphere."

Kastan, David Scott, "*All's Well That Ends Well* and

the Limits of Comedy," in *ELH*, Vol. 52, No. 3, Autumn 1985, pp. 575-89.

> Kastan argues that, although *All's Well That Ends Well* and Shakespeare's other "problem plays" are classified as comedies and not tragedies because "fictive aspirations have been gratified," the reader is not entirely satisfied with these "aspirations" and indeed has been "made suspicious of them," thus making the plays "generic mixtures" or "mutations."

Makaryk, Irene Rima, "The Problem Plays," in her dissertation, *Comic Justice in Shakespeare's Comedies*, 1979.

> Makaryk discusses *All's Well That Ends Well* within the context of the two other "problem plays" with which it is usually aligned—*Measure for Measure* and *Troilus and Cressida*.

Maus, Katharine Eisaman, "*All's Well That Ends Well*," in *The Norton Shakespeare*, edited by Stephen Greenblatt, W. W. Norton, 1997, pp. 2175-81.

> Maus's essay provides an overview of *All's Well That Ends Well*, touching on such topics as the reversal of gender roles, the lack of "endings" in the play, desire, honor,

and social class.

Muir, Kenneth, "*All's Well That Ends Well*," in *Shakespeare's Comic Sequence*, Liverpool University Press, 1979, pp. 124-32.

> Muir's article gives a brief overview of *All's Well That Ends Well*, focusing on the actions and motivations of Helena and Bertram.

Richard, Jeremy, "'The Thing I Am': Parolles, the Comedic Villain, and Tragic Consciousness," in *Shakespeare Studies*, Vol. 18, Burt Franklin & Co., Inc., 1986, pp. 145-59.

> Richard's article demonstrates how the character of Parolles fits into Shakespeare's development of the metamorphosis of the comedic villain in his work: "Parolles and the manner in which he suggests that all is not well that ends well creates a new Shakespearean drama of the pitfalls of the mental world rather than the pratfalls of the physical."

Roark, Christopher, "Lavatch and Service in *All's Well That Ends Well*," in *Studies in English Literature, 1500–1900*, Vol. 28, No. 2, Spring 1988, pp. 241-58.

> Roark argues that examining the role of Lavatch, the clown, can add an important dimension to understanding the play, especially its

more problematic elements, such as the unsatisfying ending.

Schroeder, Lori, "Riddles, Female Space, and Closure in *All's Well That Ends Well*," in *English Language Notes*, Vol. 38, No. 4, June 2001, p. 19.

> Schroeder examines the concept of female sexuality in the play from various angles and comments on the significance of pregnancy in terms of the plot and the play's title.

Simpson, Lynne M., "The Failure to Mourn in *All's Well That Ends Well*," in *Shakespeare Studies*, Vol. 22, 1994, pp. 172-88.

> Simpson examines the Oedipal anxieties in Helena and Bertram as they pertain to the failure of each to mourn the death of her/his father. Helena substitutes Bertram for her dead father, and Bertram substitutes the King of France for his. Simpson takes a psychoanalytic approach with regard to the concepts of guilt, death, forgetting, memory, and forgiveness in the play.

Snyder, Susan, "*All's Well That Ends Well* and Shakespeare's Helens: Text and Subtext, Subject and Object," in *English Literary Renaissance*, Vol. 18, No. 1, Winter 1988, pp. 66-77.

> Snyder examines two aspects of *All's Well That Ends Well* as they relate to

Helena. The first concerns the "gaps, disjunctions, and silences" in the play, "where we lack an expected connection or explanation in the speeches or actions" of Helena, primarily as they concern her character's mixture of initiative and passivity. In the second part of the essay, Snyder compares the Helena of *All's Well* with the Helena of *A Midsummer Night's Dream* and with Helen of Troy, demonstrating how *All's Well's* Helena, even at the end of the play, stands in marked contrast to the other two similarly named heroines as undesired subject rather than desired object.

Styan, J. L., *All's Well That Ends Well*, Shakespeare in Performance Series, Manchester University Press, 1984.

Styan describes how *All's Well That Ends Well* has been performed primarily on stage but also on television in the twentieth century. The first part addresses issues of performance; the second part takes the play scene by scene; and the appendix contains listings of twentieth-century productions, major productions, and principal casts.

Sullivan, Garrett A., Jr., "'Be This Sweet Helen's Knell, and Now Forget Her': Forgetting, Memory, and Identity in *All's Well That Ends Well*," in *Shakespeare Quarterly*, Spring 1999, p. 51.

> Sullivan explores the theme of lost fathers, unrequited love, and the benefits of repressed memories in the play.

Vaughn, Jack A., "*All's Well That Ends Well*," in *Shakespeare's Comedies*, Frederick Ungar Publishing Co., 1980, pp. 153-59.

> Vaughn provides a very brief overview of *All's Well That Ends Well*, touching on the difficulty critics face in assessing the motives and actions of Helena, Bertram, and Parolles. Also provides a brief stage history.

Wells, Stanley, "Plays of Troy, Vienna, and Roussillon: *Troilus and Cressida, Measure for Measure*, and *All's Well That Ends Well*," in *Shakespeare: A Life in Drama*, W. W. Norton, 1995, pp. 234-44.

> Wells's article follows the relationship of Helena and Bertram in *All's Well That Ends Well* to illuminate the play's "moral self-consciousness."

Yang, Sharon R., "Shakespeare's *All's Well That Ends Well*," in *The Explicator*, Vol. 50, No. 4, Summer 1992, pp. 199-203.

> Yang briefly explores the parallels

between the characters of Lavatch and Bertram, particularly how Lavatch's "words and experiences expose the absurdity of Bertram's perspective."

CPSIA information can be obtained
at www.ICGtesting.com
Printed in the USA
FSHW010838310319
56832FS